Annie
OAKLEY

Lucy Lethbridge is a freelance
journalist and literary editor of the
Tablet. She lives in Camden, London.
Her other book in the WHO WAS...
series, *Ada Lovelace: Computer
Wizard of Victorian England*,
won the Blue Peter Award in 2002.

WHO WAS...

Annie
OAKLEY

Sharpshooter of the Wild West

LUCY LETHBRIDGE

✳ SHORT BOOKS

First published in 2004 by
Short Books
15 Highbury Terrace
London N5 1UP

10 9 8 7 6 5 4 3 2 1

A CIP catalogue record for this book
is available from the British Library.

ISBN 1-904095-60-7

Printed in Great Britain by
Bookmarque Ltd, Croydon, Surrey.

For Oliver, Milly, Felix and Joe

CHAPTER ONE: Heading out West

One hundred and fifty years ago, the region of Darke County in the state of Ohio was known as the Wilds. It was not as wild as the frontier territory of the far West but it was a place of dark woods and dripping trees. For thousands of years, long before the white men had come and built their log cabins and cleared the woods for their cornfields, Darke County had been inhabited only by native tribes such as the Chippewas, the Ottawas, Pottawattomies, Shawnees, Delawares, Kickapoos and Eel Rivers. And their ancient tribal spirit still hung thick in the air.

The Moses family came to Darke County just before their fifth child was born in the summer of

1860: this was Phoebe Ann, otherwise known as Annie. The Moses came from the green slopes of Pennsylvania in the East, where they had kept a dirt-poor inn for travellers. Annie's parents, Jacob and Susan Moses, were not lucky, and they had struggled to make a living. When the inn had burned down, they had upped sticks, piled their children and their few remaining belongings into a handcart and headed off westward: down the Ohio River by steamboat. They intended to try their luck in a new land where they had heard that the soil was so rich you could plant a dry stick and it would sprout green leaves as big as umbrellas.

In America, in the early nineteenth century, steamboats were the only way to travel long distances. They chugged their way slowly along America's great rivers, their huge wheels churning the water into foam. Every day, the boats steamed out of the river cities of Pittsburgh and Louisville, carrying the poor, the brave, the desperate, the adventurous, and families like the Moses who wanted to begin their lives again in undiscovered country.

Steamboats were so big that in the first-class

apartments there were dining rooms and even ballrooms and viewing platforms on top. Third-class passengers like the Moses had to put up with the musty, cramped quarters of below-decks. But, through the portholes, they could gaze out at the mighty Ohio River. It was sluggish, silver and so wide that the far side was a haze. Hickory* trees and sugar maples nodded on the river banks which were hung with a dense green fringe of foliage. Sometimes there was a rustling in the greenery – a possum, maybe, or a ground-hog with long front teeth, or a black and white racoon. It might even be a wolf or a bear, because there were plenty of those, too, in the Ohio woods. It was always hot summer on the steamboats because during the winter the river was iced-up and nothing could travel up or down.

Like many people from Pennsylvania, the Moses family belonged to a religious group called the Quakers. They believed in simple living, and were sober and God-fearing. They always dressed in plain

* For an explanation of words marked with a star, see the glossary at the back of the book

grey or black. They didn't brawl or drink or swear. Quakers lived in small communities where everyone, boss or servant, was addressed equally as "brother" or "sister". Jacob Moses was a man of strong faith and he was humble, too; he was many years older than his wife, and his face was lined like an old parchment with worry. But Jacob believed that down the Ohio River there was a better life waiting for the family.

After travelling for nearly a week on the steamboat, the Moses disembarked at a tributary of the Ohio called the Stillwater, to continue their journey on a smaller vessel, an old-fashioned flatboat. Their destination was the town of Greenville, deep inside the woods.

"Look out for injuns!" said Jacob Moses, as the flatboat passed silently down the smooth and muddy river.

The Moses children watched the banks for a glimpse of a feathered headdress and listened for the zing of an arrow leaving a bow. (In those days, the Native American tribes of America were known as Indians – or "Injuns" – because when Christopher Columbus had arrived in the continent nearly five hundred years before, he thought he had come to India.) But everything was quiet. Indians were rarely seen now in Darke County: nearly 70 years earlier, in 1793, the Indians had signed a treaty at Greenville fort and divided their land between their tribes and the invaders. Now they kept themselves apart from the white farmers and stayed in their own villages.

Before long, Jacob and Susan found some land near the tiny settlement of North Star, about 20 miles from Greenville. The farmers here grew rough buckwheat, oats and beets to feed the cattle and pigs. But, most of all, this was corn country. The Indians cultivated hundreds of different kinds of corn and at harvest time the leafy plants with their silk-fringed cobs grew as tall as a man. They grew not just the yellow sweet-corn variety but white, red and even blue cobs, too. The farmers learned from the Indians how to tap the sweet, syrupy sap of the sugar maple tree by inserting spouts into the tree trunk. There were wild bees, wild grapes, wild cats and wild turkeys.

But there were also terrors: poisonous copperhead snakes and rattlesnakes, wolves and bears. In the winter the snow was so deep that people were sometimes trapped inside their homes for months, lighting bear-oil lamps against the swirling blizzards outside. The summers were so hot that the air lay shiftless over the land like a blanket and the streams dried up.

And then there were the squirrels to contend with – thousands and thousands of them and all of them pests: red ones and grey ones, eating everything in sight. Strong, chewy squirrel meat was on the menu at most meals – roasted, stewed and in pies.

CHAPTER TWO: Hard, hard work

Like all pioneers, the Moses family worked their backs to breaking to make the land provide for them. The first thing they had to do was build themselves a cabin out of logs and cultivate the swampy land for food.

The nearest small township was Woodland. The Moses bought a pair of oxen to plough the land and some cows, one of which, called Pink, became a favourite family pet. They grew apples, peaches, pears, cabbages, green beans, beets, turnips and potatoes. The animals fed on corn cobs and so did the family: their staple winter food was a kind of porridge, known as hominy grits, made from corn ground up and mixed with milk. Sometimes they would take corn kernels and throw them into a hot pan where they would burst with a loud crack and swell into delicious puffballs. This was a traditional Indian food but the white settlers named it popcorn. From spring to autumn, Susan Moses would bottle fruit and vegetables to keep in the larder during the winter; in the barn there were rows of drying apples on slatted wooden shelves. The family's only cash income was the few dollars that Jacob earned from delivering the mail by horse from North Star to the town of Woodland.

Eventually there were seven Moses children – two of them born after Annie. They never went to school as they were needed to work on the farm and they spent much of their time among the beeches and buckeye* trees, picking berries, hazelnuts, scaly-shelled hickory nuts and mushrooms. By the time she was four, Annie knew every path through the woods as though they were lines on her own hand.

For hours she would watch her mother bending over a boiling copper vat of dirty washing, pausing sometimes to push her palms into her aching back. Susan Moses was still in her thirties, but her body was curved into the shape of a comma through hard work.

14

Her face was thin and her teeth black pegs. But Susan still laughed and sang in the spring, and when she wasn't too tired she would play a game of tag with the children, pulling them under her old apron when she caught them. Annie sometimes looked at her mother's red raw fingers and understood that whatever happened in the future, one thing would always be true: life was hard, hard work. Years later, when Annie was richer than she could ever have imagined, she always remembered her mother's chafed hands in the washtub.

Every night, all the family sat together in the candlelight and prayed that God would take care of them.

"Pa," said Annie, "if the harvest fails or if squirrels eat all our vegetables or Pink don't give enough milk does that mean God ain't takin' care of us?"

"It means it's partly the weather and partly we ain't working hard enough to make it work and partly it's that owd' devil bad luck."

"So howz' God come into it?"

"God," said her father, in a voice that stopped that kind of talk dead in its tracks, "moves in mysterious ways."

At night, while outside the owls hooted, Jacob would tell the children stories. The ones they loved best were the stories of the Wild West. "If you travel down the great rivers as far as you can go, then you're in the West," whispered Jacob in the darkness. "It's strange country down there, but a poor man can make his fortune. Up in the mountains there are veins of gold as thick as your arm if you know where to look for them. And the grasslands are as rich as milk and honey. There are so many millions of buffalo that the ground shakes when they're on the move."

In their cosy wooden bed, the Moses children shivered when they imagined the West. Jacob told them about the covered wagons that made the long trail out to the great plains, and the dusty red deserts that awaited them there, where wild dogs would eat the wagons' buffalo hide coverings or a deadly rattlesnake bite your ankles. And not only deserts. "You can freeze solid in the Rocky Mountains. As high as the moon those mount'ns are, and full of strange beasts. Only fur-trappers and outlaws dare live up there and they eat nothing but berries and wolf-meat."

Despite the hard work and the struggles, Annie

had many happy memories of her childhood: the delicious-smelling smoke of a hickory wood fire; picking berries, hazels and butternuts* in the woods; feeding Pink with her soft muzzle and damp nose; listening out for Indians – hoping that they might meet one who could tell them all the secrets of the forest. But, for Annie, the best fun of all was following her father or her oldest brothers when they went hunting. Jacob Moses was a fine shot, his hands were firm and delicate and he could hit a moving target, say a squirrel, or even a tiny bird, from a hundred paces away. Annie loved the sound of her feet on the earth, padding through the undergrowth, watching for a target. "You see that," her father whispered to her once, when he shot a quail, "always hit a beast clear through the head – it keeps the meat clean of the taste of gunpowder."

No good Ohio farmer back in those days wasted a single thing: "Never put your trust in the future because no one knows what the future will bring," was their motto, and they had to make sure there were supplies to last them through the hard months. There was nothing on the farm that couldn't be re-used as something else, and when something had been patched and beaten and re-shaped until there was no more use in it, it would go into the stove for fuel. When Jacob killed a cow it wasn't just for the family's pot. He tanned its hide for clothes and shoes, stretching the cowskin till it was supple then hanging it up to dry in the barn where it flapped from the rafters like a giant tobacco leaf. The hide of one cow made waistcoats, belts, bags and shoes for all the family.

Then in the winter of 1865, when Annie was five, disaster struck. It was bitter weather, with a snow blizzard howling round the cabin where the family huddled round the wood stove. Only Jacob was out in the cold, riding back from Woodland where he had been to fetch supplies.

The family waited in the warm for their father to return. Susan kept singing hymns to keep their spirits up but the children could see that she was worried sick and kept nervously rubbing her red hands together over the stove and looking at the door

"Put another log in the stove," she said, "your father will be home soon with the horses and he'll need warming." They waited and waited, but there was no sign of Jacob. The hours passed, and the younger ones, including Annie, were sent to bed where they lay awake listening for horses' hooves.

Then around midnight there was a sound outside, a whinnying and stamping muffled by snow. Susan rushed to the door and pulled it open. There outside was their father's horse, freezing cold, its blue lips pulled back over chattering teeth.

Annie slipped out of bed and through the open door she saw the starlight bright as diamonds on the snow, and she saw the horse, and on top of the horse she saw Jacob. He was stiff as a board, frosted over and ghost white, his hands gripping the reins as though they were riveted there by icicles. He couldn't speak and he couldn't move: the blizzard had stolen his voice, leaving only a gulping, crying noise. When they pulled him off the horse he was so ramrod-stiff that it seemed as if he might snap in two. Annie's brothers took the horse into its warm stable while Susan led their father to a chair near the fire.

He did thaw out eventually and moved and talked again – but from that night on Jacob was an old man, sitting by the fire in all seasons, rubbing his bony, transparent hands as if he feared he would never be warm again. He was 62 years old, with a rheumy cough, and lungs that wheezed like bellows with a hole in them. A year later, he got pneumonia and died, leaving Susan Moses to bring up her seven children on her own.

CHAPTER THREE: Annie and the Wolves

When Jacob died, the Moses had to find another home as now they had even less money than before. Susan found a nearby cabin which she leased from kindly neighbours and she found work as a local nurse for the district. She was paid $1.25 a week.

Susan was popular with the neighbours and they were kind to the family. They said to each other: "That's a whole-souled* woman – always smilin' and lookin' on the bright side and after all the trials she's bin through..." Sometimes they invited the children in and gave them a cookie each – or a nickel for watching the horses.

But Annie, not yet seven, wanted to go hunting, to

tramp through the undergrowth again as she had done with her father. She confided in a neighbouring farmer's wife, who made clear her disapproval. "It ain't ladylike dear, a little scrap like you firing off a gun. It's men's work, hunting for food, and the job of women is to cook it up for 'em. That's the way it is and the way it always will be. Even the heathen injuns don't have their women goin' out shootin' wild beasts."

But Annie was not to be deterred. She started laying traps for small animals in the way that Jacob had taught her. She made them out of stiff cornstalks tied upright together with string like tiny log houses. Then she placed them on the ground and dug trenches underneath into which a small bird or animal would fall when it walked into the stalk cage. This way she caught dozens of little birds which Susan cooked up in stews.

One day, when there was no one in the house, Annie climbed up on a chair and pulled down her father's old-fashioned Kentucky rifle from its hooks above the fireplace. She could barely carry it, it was almost as long as she was, but she managed to take it outside and rest it on her shoulder. It felt as comfortable as if it was especially made to sit there. Then, seeing the white tail of a rabbit in the field, she looked down the barrel of the gun and pulled the trigger – crack! Bull's-eye! That night the family sat down to rabbit pie.

Susan, like the farmer's wife, did not approve of Annie shooting. It didn't feel quite right: she was only seven years old after all. But she had to admit that Annie had a knack for it; she rarely missed her target. Out into the woods she would go, heaving that great gun on her small shoulder and back she would come with a squirrel for the pot. "That child has an eye like a gimlet," said the neighbours. "Lawks... she could thread a needle a mile away!"

But although the Moses had plenty to eat, in other ways their fortunes worsened. Susan realised that she could no longer afford to keep them all together and she sent the younger children to live with neighbouring families who agreed to look after them until things looked up.

When Annie was eight, she was sent off to the Darke County Infirmary, known to people round Greenville, as the "poor farm". Anyone from around those parts who was destitute or orphaned ended up in the poor farm.

Annie travelled there in the back of a horse and cart, her few clothes and belongings tied up in a strip of cloth. Through the woods and the fields, the sun was beating down and there was a morning mist over the dry mud track. The Poor Farm was situated just outside Greenville, a redbrick building three storeys high. It was bigger than any place Annie had ever seen.

She was greeted at the door by a woman with a knot of hair and a bony head on a large, comfortable body. Annie didn't think she looked too bad – not as bad as she'd imagined anyway. This was Mrs Nancy Ann Edington, the superintendent of the Infirmary, and Annie was to lodge with her and her husband Samuel in their rooms. She had a wooden truckle bed in the corner of their kitchen but that night was the first time she had slept in a bed on her own: at home on the farm all the seven children had slept in just two beds, top to toe like pilchards* in a tin.

The Edingtons were kind people, and Quakers too, like the Moses. Samuel wore simple grey and black, just as Jacob had done, and they addressed each other as brother and sister. All was quiet and orderly in the Infirmary and although the poor and orphaned children had threadbare clothes, they were clean and had plenty to eat, and they learned skills that would bring them some pin* money when they went into the outside world.

That first day, Mrs Edington took Annie downstairs and showed her the wooden tables where children sat in rows sewing or working at their lessons; they eyed her watchfully. Down in the kitchen some more children were podding lima* beans and others sat on the floor playing jacks with knuckle bones.

"Why Annie, don't look so scared," said Mrs Edington, "you ain't an orphan, there is a chance for you to make summat good for yourself. You gotta learn how to bring in some money for your poor ma."

So Annie learned to sew. She patched, stitched and darned and earned a few cents mending the orphans' clothes. She was nimble and soon she could sew a seam plumb-straight and patch a jacket so you couldn't spot the joins. Mrs Edington was impressed by how hard she concentrated. Annie was a worker: she knew that if she was to look after her family she had to sew till her fingers were bleeding. She liked sitting by the window with her needle and thread, looking at the hills outside the infirmary and watching snipe flying in zig-zags across the marsh.

One day, a man came to the Infirmary and told Mrs Edington he was looking for a young girl to look after their new baby while his wife was busy with house-work and the other children; he said he'd pay good wages. When Mrs Edington led him into the kitchen, Annie heard the sound of his steel-capped boots on the stone floor. He was very tall, and his face was sallow and whiskery. It was customary then for men to have bushy beards or sideburns shaped like mutton-chops; they didn't set much store by shaving in the farms of Ohio. Annie could see his mouth inside his beard and his lips were red and thin. But he seemed friendly enough; he smiled and said he'd take Annie if she'd like to come with him. "I'll send you to the schoolhouse," he promised her, "and they'll teach you letters."

Well, that clinched it for Annie: she wanted to read and write and she saw this could be a chance to learn.

Although she was nearly nine, Annie had never been to school. There were few books at the Moses's home although when Jacob was alive he had often read aloud from the family Bible. Annie remembered his gnarled finger marking the lines as he worked his way down the page.

That evening, when Annie had driven away with the man to his farmstead, Mrs Edington penned a letter to Susan: "It's a respectable family I am sure," she wrote, "and their farm is fruitful. I've heard that they are quite wealthy with several acres of land. Annie will have a fine time with them." (No one knows the name of this family because, although Annie wrote about them in her autobiography many years later, she referred to them only as the "Wolves". That gives us a pretty good idea of what kind of people they were.)

The farm was white-painted, with neat fences and tubs of flowers, and the "She-Wolf", as Annie called her, was a pretty woman, plump and well-fed with hands that didn't look as though they toiled at the laundry. The children were spoiled with painted, shop-bought toys that Annie would have liked to play with too.

But Annie never got to play with any toys. And she never got to go to school either. For the first month, everything seemed to go fairly smoothly. The She-Wolf said elaborate thank-yous whenever Annie did anything. Annie thought this was strange – after all they were paying her to work. Once she offered Annie a sickly cake from a fancy box. "Go on Annie!" she laughed with all her teeth showing, "have one – it ain't gonna poison ya." But Annie wouldn't touch it. She'd never eaten candy before and she distrusted this woman with her sugary smiles.

Every day, from the house, Annie watched the local children walking down the lane carrying their school slates. When Annie timidly mentioned going to school herself, the She-Wolf replied, "Of course you'll be attendin' school Annie. Though why you want to go to school I just do not undertand. Why, I can teach you as well as any schoolroom spinster and you'll only bring home nits from those horrid children."

But as the months went by Annie never went to school – not once. She earned fifty cents a week which she sent straight to Susan to help the family, but she was little more than the Wolves' slave. After a while, the She-Wolf stopped pretending to be kind and acted peevish and spoilt. Annie rose at four in the morning to prepare breakfast for the family, then she milked the cows, washed the dishes, skimmed the milk, fed the livestock, weeded the garden, gathered wild fruit and looked after the baby. Her only peaceful time was in the woods, among the birds and the toadstools, laying traps for animals for the family's stew-pot.

Annie hated and feared the Wolves. She shrank from She-Wolf's high-pitched whine, but most of all she dreaded the He-Wolf and the heavy tread of his boots at the door when he returned home. Once, when Annie fell asleep over her darning, the She-Wolf yanked her by the hair and threw her outside into the snow.

"I was slowly freezing to death..." Annie wrote later, remembering her father and the ice knives that had killed him. Her employers brought her inside eventually but she was so ill that she lay tossing and turning feverishly in her bed the next morning – and was given nothing to eat. Sometimes the He-Wolf beat her so hard that for weeks her shoulders were stained all over with black and green bruises. And during all this time, the Wolves wrote regularly to Susan that Annie was happy and doing well at school.

Annie lived with the Wolves for two years, until she was eleven: to be precise, until one April day when the family were all away from home. The day was bright and blue with a happy, hopeful, springtime kick to it and Annie was hanging out the washing. As the sheets billowed in the sun, she thought – "I could run away!"

Annie didn't know where the Wolves' farm was because she had never been allowed outside its boundaries. She only knew that the nearest town was to the east of the house. She had seen the wagons rattling past on their way to deliver goods there, so she reckoned she knew in which direction she should be heading. She finished hanging up the washing, cleaned the stove, made her bed, left the front-door key in a tin cup and started off down the road, walking fast, not daring to look back.

The road was clotted with mud in deep ruts and walking was difficult. Annie's boots were soon coated with filth and the hem of her dress splashed with dirty water from puddles. But after only two hours walking straight, following the maple trees along the side of the road, she came to a town of wooden and brick houses. Bold as brass she headed down the main street, her eyes fixed on the end of it, and the railroad station which lay just outside the town. Annie had never seen a train but she could hear the loud hiss of the steam engines and the bell which rang, "All aboard!".

Mrs Edington, who had been on a train, had told her about fine society on its way to the great stations of St Louis and Chicago and New York. This town had a proud, shiny look to it: the houses looked new-built and there was a hotel with velvet curtains in the windows. This town seemed to say: "Look at us! We are not a two-dime piece of nowhere. We are a rail-road stop on the big new map of America...!"

The station was crowded out with ladies in hooped crinolines* of turkey red and indigo blue, and gentlemen in loud check suits. There were crates and packages in piles all over the platform. "This plunder* headin' West?" Annie heard a porter say as he heaved a box into the train.

Heading West! Annie wondered what it could contain. Silks for the ladies on the frontier maybe or fine

31

French wines or bales of calico or beads and mirrors to trade for skins with the tribes on the plains. She remembered how her father used to say that the West was a paradise, how if he was younger he would have taken his family on the Oregon Trail to the very frontier of civilisation, where a man could farm his own rolling hills as far as the horizon. And now this steaming, belching, fire-breathing iron dragon was taking its cargo of hopeful passengers all the way to the West – to begin their lives all over again in new country, under a big sky. And along the way, it could take Annie home – away from the Wolves and on to the beginning of the rest of her life.

She sprang up the metal steps, into a carriage fitted with wooden benches, and sat down by an open window just as the train began to pull away. Sitting beside her was a gentleman in a dusty black suit with a tie made from a bootlace. The man winked at her.

"You vamoosed?*" he said. Annie told him everything about her getaway: he was the first kind person she had met for two years. She was embarrassed to tell her new friend she couldn't read the station signs, so she asked him to wake her up when they got to the stop nearest to Woodland; then she snoozed as if she had a lifetime of sleep to catch up on.

"You got any dough?" said the man. "28 cents," said Annie. "That ain't gonna get you no place. You gonna need a heap more'n that," and he reached into his pocket and pulled out a whole one-dollar note which he presented to her.

Annie got off the train at the stop nearest to the small township of Woodland and walked home to North Star. It took three hours but they were just about the happiest hours of her whole life so far. Annie was back in her own territory and she could smell the familiar scents of spring in the woods.

When she arrived at Susan Moses' log cabin, however, she could see immediately that all had not been well with the family. The house was cared for, but it was shabby and the gaps in the fence had been mended so many times that it now resembled a woody thicket. After her two years at the Wolves' farm, with their white-painted window sills and coloured curtains, Annie had forgotten how threadbare her home was and she felt the tears pricking.

When Susan opened the door, she was wearing her

grey Quaker dress as she always did, and her simple white cap. She looked worn and tired but when she saw Annie her eyes opened wide with surprise and she lit up smiling. Annie was so glad to see her that she almost fell through the front door. And she would have flung herself into her mother's arms on the spot had Susan's arms not been occupied with a two-legged woollen bundle. A baby!

While Susan stroked her face, Annie just stared and stared. Then she noticed that behind her mother, inside the cabin, was a tall shadow of a man wearing dark working clothes. "Annie," said Susan, "this baby is Emily, your half-sister," and then, beckoning him out onto the porch, "this is my husband Joseph Shaw, your new pa."

CHAPTER FOUR: The first shooting match

Annie was so happy to be home that at first she was barely aware of the changes that had afflicted her family. But soon she learned that times had been hard for them.

Her mother had married not just once since Jacob died but twice; her second husband had died soon after their wedding; then Susan herself had suffered from typhoid and nearly died. And now Annie's new stepfather Joseph had hurt his knee which prevented him from working in the fields. On top of everything else, Susan and Joseph had been robbed by a scoundrel who had cheated them into handing over much of their land for a loan.

Joseph was a big, gentle man – it seemed that for all

his bulk he would tremble like an aspen tree if a strong wind blew. He wasn't a match for an unscrupulous shyster*. Annie liked her new stepfather and he taught her to read and write – because what Joseph liked doing more than anything was reading, history books especially. She learned the alphabet quickly but she was twelve years old before she had really mastered reading.

The Moses were happy to be together as a family again, though it meant meagre food rations and five of them in one bed. But after about a year it became clear to Annie that she had to earn some more money. In those days, it was quite normal for children to go out to work: most poor families had no choice. So Annie took her courage in her hands and left home for the second time, to return to Mrs Edington and the Greenville Infirmary. The Edingtons were as kind as ever and they took her into their family, encouraging her with her reading, and giving her work sewing clothes for the orphans. She stitched hundreds of dresses and knitted as many comforters*, as well as doing the stocktaking in the kitchens which meant making a list of all the goods that are in stock and ordering supplies of household foods such as butter and cream, and kerosene for the oil lamps.

For two years Annie stayed with the Edingtons, carefully putting aside a few cents every week so that she soon had some savings. All her life Annie was careful with money; even when she had earned a pile, she took care not to spend it all but to keep some in the bank. More than anything else she feared poverty and in later years she gave away much of her money to orphaned or poor children. She never forgot what it was like to scrimp and scratch a living.

By the time she left the Poor Farm at Greenville, Annie was fourteen years old. She was still small for her age, but she had a neat, muscular figure, with long brown hair which she wrapped in curling rags at night to make it wavy. Her face was not exacty pretty but it was full of character with strong, determined eyebrows and big, fierce dark eyes. She had agile fingers that hours of sewing in straight lines had made firm and steady.

Annie loved working with her hands but what she wanted to do more than anything was to shoot. Sometimes, in the long hours at the Poor Farm, she had looked out of the window at the woods and wished that she was walking through the undergrowth with her rifle. Whenever she had felt lonely or homesick it was the crackle of the leaves underfoot or the autumn smell of toadstools among the trees near North Star that she had dreamed about.

On her return home, she practised with her father's gun whenever she had a chance, bringing home wild turkeys, quail, snipe and squirrels for the family. She spent some of her savings on two linsey* dresses with matching knickerbockers, a cap, some mittens, some thick yarn stockings and a pair of copper-toed boots. She also bought animal traps, gunpowder and shot.

At first light every morning she was out in the woods looking for game. It was during this time that Annie learned that she was ambidextrous – which means that she could shoot (and do anything else, including writing) equally well with her right and her left hand.

Annie sold anything extra from her game bag to Mr Leopold Katzenberger who owned the general store in Greenville where she bought her ammunition. Mr Katzenberger was tickled pink by Annie – when she came into the store, he would call out: "Hey half-pint, who you shootin' at today?" or "Hey Mizz dead-shot, I'm mindin' my bee-haviour with you holding that big rifle there at my head!"

Annie's game was in such demand that Mr Katzenberger shipped it out to the big cities. It was preserved in salt, packed in barrels and sent down the railroads to the swanky hotels of Chicago and St Louis. Mr Katzenberger would chuckle mightily at the thought of some dandy city swell* sitting down to a dish of broiled* quail or rabbit stew little guessing that it came courtesy of a modest-mannered, fourteen-year-old girl in the Ohio backwoods. For Christmas he gave Annie two boxes of percussion caps, five pounds of shot and a can of DuPont Eagle Ducking Black Powder – the finest gunpowder money could buy.

It was Annie's earnings which saved her family from ruin – even though Annie's two older sisters had married and left home which took some strain off the family's finances. Poor mild Joseph was going blind and the children took it in turns to read his history books to him. Susan was terrified of what would happen to them, but Annie was able to hand over a heap of chinking, clinking coins every week. The Moses would not starve.

One day, when Annie was fifteen, she strolled into Mr Katzenberger's store for supplies. "Hey young crack-shot..." he called out, "Whoah Mizz Splice-a-Dice. How'd ya like to win yourself a prize?" It turned out that Mr Katzenberger had had a visit from one Jack Frost, owner of a Cincinnati hotel which was supplied with Annie's game. "I was tellin' him about how there was nothin' you couldn't shoot, bim* on target, and says Mr Frost, 'She oughta go in for a shooting match!' Well it got me thinkin' – there's big prize money in shooting matches Annie..."

"I dunno... Maybe," said Annie.

"Mr Frost says that there's a famous shooter stayin' in Cincinnati, Annie. I reckon you'd have a chance of lickin' him in a contest. Why dontcha try?"

Annie would say nothing more on the matter, but that night, at home, she thought about it hard. And the more she thought about it the more it seemed a good idea. She had never shot at the metal disc known as a "clay pigeon" before; it sprang out of a machine known as a trap. Annie had only ever shot real animals, and only for food (she would never have shot an animal just for sport). But she knew that she had a sharp eye and a sure hand. Why not try her luck in a competition?

The next day, she told Mr Katzenberger that she wanted to challenge the Cincinnati shooter to a match. He delightedly telegraphed Jack Frost to make the arrangements. Let the famous shooter come out to Darke County and see what a surprise the folk there could spring on him!

Shooting matches were very popular entertainment in America at that time, with champion shooters travelling all over the country to demonstrate their skills, to win big prizes and be treated like royalty. But Annie had lived all her life in the backwoods and she had never been to a shooting match. She knew nothing about the flashy world of the celebrity shooters. The name of her opponent was still a mystery, but the news that Annie was to challenge a famous shooter to a match spread fast around North Star and the local people (to whom nothing so exciting had happened for years) speculated excitedly about who he might be:

"Mebbe it's Captain Adam Bogardus, Annie, the champion shooter of the whole entire world."

In fact, the mystery shooter's name was Mr Francis E. Butler, known as Frank, who bragged to his audiences that he could "outshoot anything living save Captain Bogardus". Frank had travelled all over America, from the mountains to the great plains, displaying his skill at hitting whirling glass balls and clay pigeons. But he was used to performing on a stage, in a theatre with velvet curtains, or a circus ring. He didn't know who or what to expect from this god-forsaken stretch of farming country miles off the railroad line.

On the train to Greenville, he spat on his silk handkerchief and gave his shining spurs a polish. He smoothed his luxuriant moustache. He was Frank Butler after all and he felt confident that he could easily beat any shooter that came out of Darke County. But he wondered nonetheless who it would be: the legendary Don Carver perhaps, who had beaten Captain Bogardus in a famous 25-day match not many miles from here?

Annie got her first glimpse of Frank as he rolled up

in Mr Katzenberger's wagon. He was looking rather green after two hours of country roads. She saw a tall man with a bushy brown moustache wearing a natty green coat and shiny boots. A large white poodle trotted at his heels and when Frank walked out in front of the crowd, the poodle sat obediently in a corner.

With a great display of pushing up his cuffs and twirling his moustache, Frank placed an apple on the dog's head. Then he walked a hundred paces off and shot it clear away with one bullet. The crowd roared with excitement.

When Annie walked out into the field – well, as Frank was later to tell the story, you could have "knocked me down with a feather". His jaw dropped: his opponent was a girl! And a very young girl at that, dressed demurely in buttoned boots and a cotton dress that came to just above her ankles, with her hair flowing down her back. He could hear the crowd whooping with delight. "Go on Annie, you show him gal!" For a moment, Frank, who was a good-hearted type, wondered if maybe he should ease up a bit, let her take a few points. He didn't want to see a young lady humiliated.

But he was a seasoned performer and when he stepped up there in front of the trap, with the cheers of the crowd ringing in his ears, he knew he was there to win. A flamboyant bow to the audience and Frank primed his rifle as the clays shot out of the trap. One! Two! Three! Four! and on he went till twenty five – all of them had to be hit with one rifle barrel. With his shooting done, Frank stepped back smiling at the cheers: twenty four hits out of twenty five; it looked like an easy victory.

Annie was damp with nerves when she took her place in front of the crowd. Everyone was silent, crossing their fingers, willing her on. Crracckk! Out shot the clays and Annie unloaded her barrel into the air. One! Two! Three! Four! … yes! … she hit that one ….! Yes and that! Mr Katzenberger shut his eyes tight (he'd gambled 20 dollars on Annie's winning this match). Twenty three! Twenty four! And…….. yes! Twenty five! Yes, yes, twenty five! A FULL SCORE! Annie had won… she had won her very first match. She had outshot Mr Francis E. Butler who could outshoot anyone in America!

Annie's prize was fifty dollars – the most money

she had ever seen in her whole life. Nobody she had ever known had ever seen that much money. The crowd went wild, throwing their hats, their handkerchiefs and their children in the air. Annie took bow after bow, her prize money safe in her inside pocket. Annie's brothers and sisters were elated: what would Susan and Joseph say when Annie came home with fifty dollars simply for doing what she did every day of the week!

Afterwards, Frank Butler came strolling up to Annie. "Well, Mizz Oakley, you had me fairly beat," he said. "It seems to me that you would certainly give Captain Bogardus himself a run for his money!" Annie observed that above the fine moustache there was a pair of bright, kindly blue eyes.

As Annie climbed into the Moses' wagon to drive home, she felt something nuzzling her skirts. It was Frank Butler's white poodle with a piece of apple in his mouth which he deposited on her lap. "Mizz Oakley," called Frank as they drove off, "you have made another conquest. Generally George is not well-disposed towards ladies but he has very plainly taken a shine to you."

Two days later, a package arrived for Annie postmarked Cincinnati. Inside was a box of candy with a message pinned to it: "*With warmest regards from George*" it read. A few days after that, the acclaimed shooter Mr Frank Butler came to North Star to call at the Moses household in person.

It seemed that George's master had also taken a shine to Annie.

CHAPTER FIVE: Annie, Frank and Sitting Bull

When he had finished his show in Cincinnati, Frank took a room in the hotel in Woodland and visited Annie every few days. They walked around the woods together and practised shooting targets which they set up on the fence. George sat patiently to attention while they shot apples and balls off the top of his head from different distances and awkward angles.

Frank told her that he'd been born in Ireland 26 years before. When he was a young child, his parents had emigrated to America, promising to send for him when they were settled. But he had never heard from them again, and aged thirteen he had sailed across the Atlantic on a steamer, working in exchange for his ticket. He described how when he arrived in New York, the quayside had been teeming with people of every nationality, all of them looking for work. He'd fallen in with a circus troupe, touring the cities of the East Coast with a menagerie of animals and human acrobats. At first he'd helped behind the scenes, fixing ropes, feeding the horses and securing tent hooks, but gradually Frank had worked his way up to his own slot in the show, an act with a dog and pony. Between scene changes, he had learned how to shoot, training his eye by firing at different targets.

So Frank had become a shooter, one of the best in America. He had travelled around the states on the railroads, bringing his act to the sparkling new cities of the American continent, to the pioneer settlements and the gold rush towns, from the prairies to the foothills of the Rocky Mountains themselves. He'd started out in "vaudeville" which means a variety of entertainments in small theatres, mostly singing and dancing.

"You shoulda seen Little Tich," he laughed, "three foot high and dancing in giant shoes!" Then he went back to the circus, to the big top extravaganzas.

"Picture it Annie," he said, "some of them are so big that they are like whole towns in themselves and when they pitch camp there are so many tents that you can't see the end of them stretchin' to the horizon."

He told her how in the circuses there were camel trains, herds of elephants and troupes of trapeze artists who could turn triple somersaults in mid-air 50 feet above the audience. "I've seen a blindfold man throw a hundred knives at a board where his wife is standin' and she's steppin' off the stage with not a scratch on her."

Although Frank had worked in all the great circuses of America, there was one show that he wanted to have a part in more than any other: "Buffalo Bill's Wild West Show, Annie. It's the greatest show on earth. There are cowboys showin' how they can lasso a gallopin' steer* and there's the Deadwood Stagecoach* that was attacked by Sioux Indians – they act that out too! With real Indians in warpaint hollerin' and real cowboys on horseback Annie – just like it is in life, only on stage nobody dies!"

Annie had spent all her life in Darke County. She had never met anyone who told stories like these. Now she too wanted to travel, to be part of the adventure of the Wild West. Frank was ten years older than Annie, he'd seen the world, but he knew when he met her, that he wanted to marry her, that she was his perfect partner. How many women can shoot a squirrel off a chimney stack at five hundred paces in twilight? A man might look all his life for such a soulmate. He asked Annie to marry him, and she of course said yes.

History tells us that Annie and Frank were married in 1876 – when Annie was sixteen. However, later in their careers they may have changed the dates because when Annie was a big star, she took six years off her age so that she always appeared to be a young girl. So although we'll go along with the line that she was married at sixteen, she might actually have been 22.

What is definitely true is that Frank was booked to appear in shows all over America during the 1870s and, after they married, whenever that was, Annie went with him. They travelled by train all over the states of the Mid-West and Annie saw the glassy waters of Lake Michigan and the lush green valleys of Kentucky. America had opened up before her.

Frank performed with a partner whose job it was to

throw glass balls into the air for him and generally to assist him by setting up the other targets. One night, when they were booked for an evening show at the Crystal Hall in Springfield, Ohio, Frank's partner fell ill and Annie suggested that she might go on instead. "You mean to hold up the objects so I can shoot at 'em?" said Frank. "Well I can do that," replied Annie, "but I can also take a crack at them myself." Well, Frank saw that there might be an advantage to this and that night, they both went on to the stage and every time Frank took a shot, Annie matched it with a shot of her own. They made the perfect team – and the applause proved it. People were not accustomed to seeing a lady shooter and it had novelty value; it looked as though Annie and Frank were the ideal double act.

Following their success in Springfield, they created a new show – which starred both of them. Annie decided to change her name too: in the world outside the stage she was known as Annie Butler, but for a stage name she wanted something memorable that rang out strong and had a touch of the forest about it. "I'm gonna be called Annie *Oakley*," she announced.

It wasn't long before Frank Butler and Annie Oakley were a regular star turn. Audiences loved the sight of little Annie with her hair flying behind her potting crack shots through playing cards (bang through the ace of the Ace of Spades!), shooting corks out of bottles or snuffing out candles.

Soon it became clear that Annie had become the star of the act. Frank was generous about this: in fact, he decided to retire from the stage and become Annie's agent and manager. Annie began to design her own stage costumes, opting for a style that she wouldn't change for nearly 50 years. Quaker Annie never approved of clothes that showed too much flesh and she always wore a dress that stopped just above her ankles, with leggings worn underneath. Mostly the dresses were made of buckskin*, which gave the audience a flavour of the pioneering Far West. She also wore buttoned-up gaiters* and sometimes a wide-brimmed hat. Her hair was always worn loose. Over the years, Annie pinned all her shooting medals to her dress and they sparkled under the lights like a polished breastplate.

In 1884, Annie and Frank signed a contract with the

Sells Brothers Circus – one of the biggest shows in the United States. The Sells circus steamed its way across the country in its own long fleet of railroad cars containing 50 cages of live animals, including an enormous elephant called Emperor, a two-horned rhinoceros and a giraffe. This was many years before the days of television and no one had seen marvellous creatures like these. Alongside Annie Oakley, the human performers included a whole family of trick cyclists, a Chinese dwarf, a lady rider called Adelaide Cordona who could stand on her head on top of a galloping horse, and high-jumper Frank Gardner – known as the "lofty Leaper".

It was long, arduous work, performing night after night, practising by day and always on the move, travelling hundreds of miles in uncomfortable trains. Behind the razzamatazz of the lights and the applause, the members of the circus were mostly unhappy and dissatisfied. They were paid a pittance and often they were not even given enough to eat. Frank and Annie, as the show's chief attractions, were slightly better treated, but they too came to regret having signed a contract with the Sells Brothers, which tied them to performing for a whole year. On winter nights, the Butlers huddled in their cold, damp tent listening to the hungry animals moaning in their cages. And, as soon as their year was up, they left – though not before Annie had made a new friend, one of the most famous characters in the story of the Wild West.

Chief Sitting Bull was the most celebrated American Indian in the world. He was chief of the Hunkpapa Sioux tribe of Dakota who had been ordered out of their ancient hunting grounds in the Black Hills when the white men had discovered gold there. The Sioux had rebelled, and refused to leave their land. And the white men had then decided to launch an attack, to punish the Indians for their resistance.

At a place called Little Bighorn in the mountains of Montana, General Custer and several hundred soldiers from the American cavalry had one day taken the Sioux warriors by surprise. But the Indians, led by Sitting Bull, had turned on their attackers and Custer and almost all his soldiers had been massacred. The Hunkpapa victory at the Battle of Little Bighorn was now the most famous battle in the West and, although the Sioux had eventually lost their fight to preserve their sacred lands, the hawk-nosed Chief Sitting Bull was a feared and admired figure. He had become a celebrity. The chief made occasional visits to the noisy encampments of the white man and when he did, from Baltimore to St Paul, people queued up for a glimpse of a real Sioux chieftain.

Sitting Bull happened to be in St Paul when Annie and Frank were performing at the city's Olympic Theatre. Watching as Annie pranced onto the stage wielding her rifle, the Chief was intrigued – and enchanted. And he decided to call on her in her dressing room.

Annie saw an old man, hair in a long pigtail, his eyes shrewd and observant, his face deeply creased by snow and sun. He sat with her for a long time, and told her the story of his people, how the Sioux were now living in special reservations, their traditional hunting grounds offering nothing but the brick dwellings of the pale-faces.

"We fought them but we lost the fight," said the Chief wearily. "Once we were safe in the lands of the West. We thought they could not follow us there. But the coming of the iron horse* has changed everything. The buffalo have gone, hunted by the white man and his guns, and the Sioux cannot live without the buffalo.

"They try to make us stop hunting and become farmers, to dress our children in smocks and send them to school to learn English. And they give the warriors of the Sioux firewater* so they can no longer fight or work."

As she listened to Sitting Bull, Annie remembered how in the years of her childhood, she had listened for the sound of an Indian footfall in the forests, for the sound of canoe paddle or the zing of an arrow. But she had heard nothing, had never met an Indian before this moment. She was fascinated by the stories that he told, of how the Sioux had lived before the white settlers had come and of the changes that the white men had brought.

Annie visited Sitting Bull many times while they were both in St Paul. Once he told her that Buffalo Bill Cody of the Wild West Show had been to see him: "He offered me many dollars to perform the Battle of Little Bighorn before a crowd of people, to kill again that strutting turkey General Custer," said Sitting Bull.

"He has taken many Indians into his show and they travel far over the horizon in the shining carriage of the Iron Horse. Every day, they must live again their battles against the white men, but now no one dies. They perform the war dances of their ancestors but they fight only shadows."

The Chief sighed. "I have lived too long for these strange times Annie. You kill your enemy in real life and then you must kill him again and again – for the pale-faces' entertainment!" Before they parted, he told her he wanted to adopt her as an honorary daughter of the Hunkpapa Sioux. And he gave her a Sioux name – *Watanya Cecilla* which in English means "Little Sure Shot".

CHAPTER SIX: The Wild West Show

Captain Adam H. Bogardus, with his glossy chestnut locks, his tight breeches and his rhine-stone encrusted gloves, was the most famous shooter in the world. No one had ever toppled Captain Bogardus from his star position in Buffalo Bill's Wild West Show. In 1869 (when Annie had been only nine years old), someone had bet him $1000 to shoot 500 pigeons in eleven hours – and he had completed the job in only nine hours. Ever since then, he had shot his way round Europe and America, waving his elegant gloves to the crowds that loved him. Now his four sons, aged between nine and nineteen were on the stage with him, too: the Bogardus family were considered unbeatable.

But now, in 1885, Captain Bogardus was tired. Enough was enough. For a quarter of a century he'd been scuffing up sawdust under the arc lights of the circus ring. How exhausting it was, maintaining such unnaturally brown hair, remembering to hold his stomach in and to keep his eye straight on the spinning glass balls. Captain Bogardus wanted to be a gentleman of leisure: it was time for Buffalo Bill to look for a new star shooter.

While Captain Bogardus dreamed of retirement, Annie was in Springfield, Ohio, practising her act for that evening's performance. She was outside in a field she used for target practice, standing on her head and firing behind her while looking in a mirror. She paused to get her breath and at that moment a short, plump man in a bowler hat ran out into the field, the sunlight glinting off his flashy watch chain.

"May I introdooce myself Mizz Oakley? I'm Nate Salsbury," he said, shaking her hand vigorously, "business partner to Colonel William H. Cody of the Wild West Show.

"I gotta tell you Mizz Oakley, that I've bin' watching you strut your stuff and I am very, very impressed.

If you woz interested, I should be delighted to offer you a part in the greatest Wild West show on earth…"

Annie acted cautious – as she always did – but she was excited when she went home and told Frank about Nate Salsbury's offer. "We shouldn't be too hasty," said Annie. But both she and Frank knew that this was their big break and they leapt at the chance.

Three days later the Butlers, accompanied by Nate Salsbury, went by railroad to Louisville, Kentucky, where Buffalo Bill himself was waiting to meet them. Or rather, he was waiting to meet *Annie*, the lady crack-shot.

Buffalo Bill was then 39 years old. He grew his hair long and loose over his shoulders in the style of a regular Western fur trapper, and he always wore a buffalo-skin jacket with long fringes like an Indian brave*; there were intricately decorated silver spurs on his boots. He was a handsome man with a fine figure and an eye for the ladies. No wonder Buffalo Bill was a star. His life had been as exciting as a story: in fact Bill's life *was* a story as he was now one of the most popular characters in bestselling novels about the Wild West.

He had left his home in the mid-West state of Kansas at the age of eleven when he got a job herding cattle. Then, still only thirteen, he drove horse-drawn wagons for pioneers who were crossing the great plains to the West. He had been a fur-trapper and a goldminer, and at the age of fourteen he had become a rider for the Pony Express – the most daring, dangerous job in America. The Pony Express delivered the mail at top speed by horseback across the West. Only the youngest, fittest men could become Express riders – and they risked their lives. No wonder the Pony Express job advertisement went like this: "YOUNG, SKINNY, WIRY FELLOWS NOT OVER 18. MUST BE EXPERT RIDERS WILLING TO RISK DEATH DAILY. ORPHANS PREFERRED".

When the invention of the telegraph had put the Pony Express out of business Bill had become an army scout, following the trails of outlaws, rogues and desperadoes to bring them to justice. Finally, he had found the job that made him his name: hunting buffalo to feed the thousands of railroad workers who were laying mile after mile of metal tracks to bring trains to every corner of America.

Buffalo Bill was the buffaloes' deadliest enemy. A buffalo is six foot from hoof to head and weighs over a ton – but Bill shot 4,280 of them in a year and a half. The plains ran with buffalo blood and their number dwindled to a fraction of what it had been before. As Sitting Bull had described to Annie, the emperor of the plains had been massacred and the plains' tribes had lost their livelihood.

Now Bill looked back with regret on his part in the end of the teeming buffalo herds of the West. He disliked the bloodthirsty hunters from the East with their great guns who took the trains out to pit themselves against the remaining beasts: he knew it was an unequal battle and he respected the Indians who knew the buffalo as a friend and who would take only the meat that they needed, leaving the buffalos to multiply for the next year.

Even so, Buffalo Bill did not spend time moping about feeling ashamed: these days he was an entertainer (and still quite prepared to exploit the buffalo if it suited him. In one act, he had a herd of buffalo appear so that everyone could see the skill with which a Sioux brave could hunt one of these great animals with only a bow and arrow. "Now there's *real* huntin'!" he used to observe from the wings.)

When Annie walked in, Bill was surprised: she was such a tiny little thing – no bigger than a prairie dog. He wondered if she'd be able to handle one of Bogardus's ten-pound shotguns.

"Well Annie – I'm gonna call you Annie as we're all family in the Wild West Show – you ain't what I'd expected. But Nate says you is somethin' special, so I'll give you a slot and see how you fare."

Buffalo Bill took out a long-stemmed clay pipe which he lit slowly: "There's a lotta people out there Annie who're claimin' to come from the West – and a lot of them are running shows too. But in my opinion, those shows are bogus, nothin' but hot air and actors dressed up: my show is the only one where it's all for real. I want folks to go away with a taste of the West like I remember it – when it was truly wild. The Wild West show's got cowboys lassooin' buckin' broncos*, and real live Indians with war dances and tomahawks* massacrin' an entire cavalry regiment. Once Indians were the enemy but in my show they're heroes as much as the other side.

"I even got a Deadwood Stagecoach – a real one – so we can tell the story of how it was attacked by Pawnees and left end-up in the sand with all its passengers murdered. We act out a buffalo hunt, a Pony Express race, the killin' of Yellow Hand the Cheyenne brave by yours truly. And we act out an attack on a settlers' cabin so realistic that I'm happy to tell you that several of the ladies in the audience have fainted durin' the action."

Bill took a puff of his pipe. "The frontier has gone – now everyone wants to recall what was in the West before we white men got there. And y'know what? I'm sad to say it's gone Annie. And I think I was one of the ones that killed it – so it is my life's duty to show people how it once was."

He sighed, "What I want is simple enough Annie. I want heroes and battles like the stories of old. I want pioneers and Indians fightin' for their lives. In short I want the smell of the mountains, plains and deserts of the great West. I don't want to see a dry eye in the house when Mizz Annie Oakley is standin' out there with her gun, a brave little lady alone in the great wilderness. You think you can give me that?"

Nate Salsbury broke in, "Bill, Mizz Oakley was tellin' me that she's gotta Sioux name meaning "Lil' Sure Shot" – it was given her by Chief Sitting Bull himself."

Buffalo Bill brightened up: "Now I like that – you put that up straight on the hoardings, Nate – the Wild West Show's own Annie Oakley 'known by her Indian name of *Little Sure Shot*'. Annie, I can see that you and me are goin' to work together just fine."

So Annie and Frank became part of the Wild West Show. In their first year with the show, they travelled right across America, performing in more than 40 cities. It was undoubtedly the biggest and flashiest entertainment in the world: when it opened in New York City, a total of 360,000 people came to watch it – 14,000 visitors every day.

The Butlers soon regarded people in the show as family. There was a lanky beanpole called Buck Taylor, "king of the cowboys", and a young whipper-snapper, Johnny Baker, the "cowboy kid" and Vernon Seavers, the "youngest cowboy in the world", who was just eight years old. The Sioux and Pawnee Indians, led by Chiefs Red Shirt and Black Elk, kept themselves apart, living in their own encampments of teepees*, but Annie got to know them well, too, and would visit the camp to play with their children. And then there was Buffalo Bill himself, known as the "Colonel". Everyone had a story about Bill, like the one about how he'd sent his wife the scalp of Yellow Hand the Cheyenne brave in a package in the mail.

"He's got a *wife*?!" said Annie to Frank, when she heard that story. "Well, yes, I believe so," said Frank, "but she's a very respectable and well-behaved lady who don't approve of the Wild West Show. So, as you can imagine, they don't see too much of each other."

The Wild West showmen were up at five every morning. They travelled by rail in coaches especially made for them; at night they put boards across the coach seats to make beds. First thing they did when they arrived at a town was pitch camp, bedding the horses down in fresh rye straw and herding the buffalo into a corral*. The show was like a moving city, slowly shifting its population across continents. Apart from the performers, there were hundreds of backstage people, such as carpenters, animal feeders and "clackers" (the people whose job it was to warm up the audience and make sure they loudly applauded). There were machines such as the giant Blower which could whip up a cyclone or a dust storm, and hundreds of animals, not just the huge herd of buffalo, but horses, dogs, and a much-loved moose* called Jerry.

In the middle of this canvas city there was the "grub tent" which served up strong coffee, steaks grilled over log fires, and eggs and beans. Mealtimes were signalled by the blaring call of a cornet. Like any city, the show community had its troublemakers and there were occasional brawls when the cowboys had had one too many whiskies. But when George, Frank and Annie's beloved white poodle, died in Toledo, everyone in the camp grieved with them. The Indian women wove wreaths of flowers and chanted into the night as George's coffin was lowered into its grave.

Each performer had their own tent but the size and splendour of it depended on their star billing. Annie had a medium-sized tent to begin with, but as her fame grew, it became an opulent, three-roomed affair with a Turkey rug and chintz (flowered) curtains; it had foldaway beds with thick blankets and a collapsible bathtub. Between shows, the Butlers sat companionably on their two folding chairs, Annie usually doing her embroidery.

Annie was up at the crack of dawn to practise firing at targets which Frank would set up for her. She worked continually to add new skills to her act. She was always a person of rigorous habit. Every morning, she ate exactly three prunes and an egg poached in milk for breakfast (she even travelled with her own iron poaching-pan); every evening, she rubbed herself down with witchhazel to soothe her muscles.

With all her exercise, she was fit and slender. While galloping bareback at full-speed, she could bend down under her horse Gipsy and untie a handkerchief from just above the horse's hoof, or scoop up her hat from the ground. She could shoot bits off a potato on a stick, piece by piece, shoot through all the diamonds in a ten-of-diamonds playing card and hit flying brass discs the size of a penny bang through the middle. She could stand on her head and fire between her knees or gallop standing-up on Gipsy while her bullets hit whirling glass balls.

Annie was such a success that she soon had a solo

spot between the Pony Express riders and Buffalo Bill himself in his famous shootout with Yellow Hand. In Annie Oakley, "the peerless wing-shot" Bill had found a star attraction.

One day a new member introduced herself in the Butlers' tent. "Howdee" came a teeny-weeny, squeaky voice. "Anybody home?" In stepped a girl, maybe fifteen years old, wearing spangly tights and a costume decorated with stars and stripes. She had dyed- blonde hair crimped into curls and was carrying a Winchester rifle.

"You Annie Oakley?" said the girl insolently, "You the one they call the Queen o' the Shooters?" Annie didn't like the look of this girl and her cocky ways.

"I'm Lillian Smith," said the girl, "a Lady Shooter also, and I jus' wanted to see whad'ya looked like." And off she went, cool as a cucumber, with her ample behind swaying from side to side. "Whoah Annie!" said Frank, "that girl's got more brass neck than a church candlestick!"

After that Annie and Lillian were competitors. For all her vulgar pizzazz, Lilian never managed to take Annie's number one position but she muscled in on a lot of attention and it has to be admitted that she could hit 25 glass balls in one minute. Gossip round the Show was that she bragged, "Annie Oakley is done for!"

Towards the end of Annie's first year with the Show, Buffalo Bill announced that he had a new recruit. "A scoop, mah friends. I've persuaded the mighty Chief Sitting Bull himself to join our operation and re-enact his victory against General Custer." Annie went to visit the old chief in his teepee. Surrounded by his wives and warriors, he was wearing his famous headdress of 40 feathers. She asked him why he was doing it.

"You know something Watanya Cecilla?" he replied, "I'm doing it for the money." He shrugged sadly. "Why not? The old days are gone. Everything is changed. The buffalo is gone, the white men's mines have made holes in our hunting grounds. What can a warrior do in these times?"

Sitting Bull leaned forward. "But I tell you this Annie. There is something rising in our people. There are rumours – a Paiute brave has seen in a vision the white people swept from our lands forever. Now the tribes dance the Ghost-Dances to summon the spirit of our ancestors to help us fight back. There will be one more battle before I die. And I can smell my death, Watanya Cecilla, the larks have warned me of it."

Sitting Bull did not stay long with the Wild West Show. He left quietly one night, saying, "The teepee is a better place. I am sick of the houses and the noises and the multitude of men."

CHAPTER SEVEN: The Wild West in London

In 1887, the Wild West Show set off on a grand European tour. They crossed the Atlantic Ocean in a ship called the *State of Nebraska*. The Deadwood Stage was locked up in the hold and cages below-decks held eighteen buffalo, ten moose, ten mules, five Texas steers, four donkeys and two deer. The Indians, who believed that travelling on water meant the end of life, chanted their death songs during a violent storm. But eventually, they arrived safely in England and set up camp in London, near Earl's Court.

Annie thought London a dirty old city, with its narrow streets and smoke-stained houses. She hated the noise of the hansom cabs (horse-drawn taxis) clattering over the old cobble-stones.

The Show took up 23 acres and there were 40,000 visitors every day day. These included Edward, the Prince of Wales, who paid a call with his wife Princess Alexandra. He was fat and jowly, with a long nose and a big cigar; his eyes bulged like gobstoppers. Annie refused to curtsey to the Prince and told him that this was because she was an American Republican, and therefore didn't approve of kings and queens. Instead she turned first to Princess Alexandra and shook her hand, saying, "because in America, ladies come first." The Prince laughed heartily, but the English audience was very shocked.

1887 was the 50th year of Queen Victoria's reign, her Golden Jubilee. The Queen had dressed in black mourning clothes since the death of her beloved husband Prince Albert in 1861. She rarely left her royal palaces and her subjects had seldom even had a glimpse of her in all that time.

Annie was amazed when Buffalo Bill ran into the Butlers' tent, brandishing a letter with a gold crest. "Y'know what this is, Sure Shot?" he shouted, "It's only a letter from her grand high Majestee herself

requestin' that we put on a special performance jus'
for her on Wednesday afternoon!"

Well. It sure was an honour. Everyone knew that
Queen Victoria had hardly been out for 26 years – and
now she wanted to come and see the Wild West Show!
Frank swept Bill a low bow: "Well Bill, you are mixin'
with the mighty!"

Behind Bill's back, though, the showmen were not
always as friendly as they had been. In the camp they
muttered that the Colonel was getting too big for
his buffalo-hide boots. He liked to sing this popular
English ditty:

> They say he's a darling, a hero
> A truly magnificent man,
> With hair that falls over his shoulders,
> And a face that's a picture to scan;
> And then he's so strong and so daring,
> Yet gentle and nice with it still –
> Only fancy if all the young ladies
> Go mashed upon* Buffalo Bill!

"Go boil your head Bill!" the Cowboy Kid yelled,

when he heard him swanking*, "If it ain't too big to fit in the saucepan!"

The Queen didn't want the hoi-polloi to be present when she came to the Show so the stadium was sealed off for the afternoon. A shiny black carriage rolled into the grounds and out stepped a retinue of ladies in crackling silk and gentlemen with black top-hats. Somewhere in the midst of them was a tiny old woman, fat as a butterball and dressed all in stiff black including her bonnet. A royal box, hung with red velvet, had been prepared and a procession of cowboys, Indians and lady shooters rode past, saluting the Queen. Buffalo Bill himself flamboyantly swept off his hat: "Welcome, Your Majesty, to the Wild West of America!"

Annie shot cigars from Frank's lips and glass balls and playing cards. She had trained Gipsy to go down on one knee and bow her head to the royal box at the end of their act. After the finale, the Queen asked Annie to step up to the box. To Annie's irritation, she also invited Lillian Smith. But it was to Annie she said: "You are a very clever little girl." Annie looked up and saw a beady old face with a long nose and bulgy eyes like Prince Edward's. "Thank you ma'am," she replied.

The Indians, who respected old people above all others, called the Queen the "Great White Mother" or "Grandmother England", and Black Elk and Red Shirt reported that she had said to them: "I am 67 years old and I have seen all kinds of people, but today I have seen the best-looking people that I know." The Queen confided to her journal that she found the show "most exciting".

While the Show was in London, Annie became one of the most popular attractions in town. Every morning she rode Gipsy in Hyde Park and a shoe-black (a child who cleaned people's shoes on the street) once cried out: "There's the boss shooter!" Hordes of children, usually accompanied by their governesses, would come to tea with the Butlers in their Earl's Court tent. The tea parties were so crowded that two policemen (Annie was delighted to find they were known as "bobbies") had to stand on either side of the entrance. Her visitors were surprised to find Annie so quiet and un-showy: after all, they had heard that her stage performance usually ended with her dramatically sliding across the ring on her stomach to secure a tricky shot. She was sent so many flowers that the tent resembled a hothouse, and also gifts of books, handkerchiefs, lace, gloves, fans and silk. On her birthday (in reality her 27th, but Annie let it be thought that she was only 21), she received more than 60 presents, including a horse, a clock, a St. Bernard puppy, a carriage and a signed photograph from Princess Alexandra.

She was also in demand for teaching gunmanship. She taught a ladies' class how to shoot at a rate of £5 a lesson (about a thousand pounds in today's money), and she and Frank were invited to grand houses for weekends where they shot pheasants in the damp English countryside. It wasn't really sport, thought Annie disapprovingly, to beat the pheasants up in the air as easy targets and then take pot shots at them.

She also took up bicycling, which she thought great fun and good exercise. In those days it was considered shocking for women to ride bicycles because they might show their legs while pedalling. Annie always wore a skirt – she was too ladylike to wear bloomers – but she devised a button on a piece of elastic so she could hook the skirt to the tops of her boots to make sure it never rode up over her knees. She always said she was the very first woman to ride a bicycle in London. Later, she incorporated bicycles into her act and would ride fast with no hands while shooting.

One day, Buffalo Bill received a letter from the Prince of Wales who wanted him to stage a shooting match between Annie and the Prince's cousin, the Grand Duke Mikhail of Russia. The Duke, who fancied himself a keen shot, wanted to marry the Prince's daughter and Prince Edward, who didn't think much of him, thought that if he was humiliatingly whipped by Annie Oakley he might slope back home to St Petersburg. Annie beat him hollow, of course: out of 50 clay pigeon targets, she hit 47 to the Duke's 36.

Meanwhile, Queen Victoria had so enjoyed her show that she decided that there should be another one, for her own private guests. All the British royal family were to be there, as well as many of the crowned heads of Europe. Bill instructed his players to fire up the stage for all they were worth for such a prodigious occasion.

"We've a regular wholesale consignment of swells

this time and we're gonna make 'em scared yellow!" he commanded, "I want yellin' and hollerin' and blood-curdlin'!"

When the royal party appeared, four European kings were invited into the Deadwood stage itself and found themselves under a gruesome attack. The Sioux pounded round the ring after the stagecoach, swinging their tomahawks and jumping through the windows. The Prince of Wales rode up on the top of the stage with Buffalo Bill and he had a wonderful time, hanging on for dear life and roaring with laughter while his roly-poly body swung from side to side. But the four kings inside were so frightened by the experience that when they finally fell out of the coach, they nearly fainted; one even vomited.

On the Fourth of July, America's Independence Day, the members of the Wild West Show had some celebrations of their own. All their new English friends were invited to a traditional American rib-roast breakfast. The cast acted as cooks, waiters and hosts. The Indians cooked the ribs of beef, stewing them slowly over a fire as was their custom, and there was stewed chicken, lobster salad, grits and hominy which Annie recalled from her long-ago Ohio childhood, as well as sweet corncobs, coconut pie, special "Wild West" apple pie, popcorn and peanuts. The Indians ate the food with white sharpened sticks while the other guests tucked in with forks and fingers.

CHAPTER EIGHT: 'Powders I have used'

The gentleman, in soldier's uniform with a big moustache like a pair of handlebars, was looking nervous. It was the Kaiser, ruler of Germany.

"I'll tell ya' one thing about Annie Oakley Your Highness," said Buffalo Bill to the Kaiser, "she don't cheat. Some o' them shooters in other shows – they got tricks. The one who makes a piano play every time he hits a target? Well, there's some mechanic backstage pullin' a handle. Or the cigar-ash trick? Sometimes there's a wire inside the cigar and the smoker pulls it to make the ash drop off.

"But that's not the way with our Annie – everythin' she hits, she hits 'cause she's got an eagle-eye and she's practised damn hard for it."

"My dear Colonel Cody," said the Kaiser, "I'm not sure I find that reassuring. I think I would prefer it if there was a little wire in my cigar."

The Kaiser was beginning to regret that he had offered to make his own cigar, clamped between his regal lips, a target for Annie Oakley. Annie had already scrambled five eggs in mid-air, shot open walnuts balanced on Frank's head and aimed back-wards by using a mirror. The Kaiser had been very impressed. But still… he closed his eyes as Annie took aim. He heard a loud crack and gingerly opened them again. His cigar was still there but its long column of ash had disappeared. "I told ya' Sir!" said Buffalo Bill clapping him on the back proudly, "She ain't no cheat – Annie's the real thing alright!"

After a year in England, the Wild West Show had begun a tour of Europe. They had visited Paris where an audience of 20,000 elegant people had awaited them. "They look kinda bad-tempered," whispered Annie backstage. But the French, who were notorious-ly hard to please, loved Annie from the moment she danced into the ring. They loved her neat costume and her flowing hair, and, of course, her skill. When her act was over the crowd roared and the auditorium was full of hats, parasols and handkerchiefs that they threw into the air.

Again she was the toast of a capital city. The King of Senegal in Africa, who was visiting Paris at the time, offered Buffalo Bill 100,000 French francs for Annie.

"Whadya want with her, Your Majesty?" said Buffalo Bill suspiciously, thinking Frank might have something to say if he sold Annie to the King.

"To destroy the tigers who cause havoc in my country's villages!" said the King. When Annie declined his offer, the king dropped to his knees and graciously kissed her hand.

After Paris, the troupe went to other parts of Europe. First to Italy, where Annie and Frank climbed the volcano Vesuvius and visited the Roman ruins at Pompeii. Then to Barcelona in Spain, and then Germany, where Annie's shooting the ash off the Kaiser's cigar made headline news all over Europe. In Germany, officers of the Prussian army, the most powerful in Europe, studied the movements of the Wild

West Show with interest. They hovered round the tented encampment scribbling notes on how such a large assemblage of men and machinery could be transported and how it pitched camp so efficiently. It certainly was impressive: eight sleeping coaches, fifteen railroad cars for stock, sixteen flatcars for equipment and 35 baggage wagons.

While they were in Europe, a false story hit the headlines of American newspapers: that Annie Oakley had died of flu in Buenos Aires. Frank and Annie telegraphed home to say it wasn't true – but Annie's mother had already cried for two days by the time she heard from them.

In 1892, Annie herself heard some sad news: Chief Sitting Bull had been killed during an uprising in the reservation of the Hunkpapa Sioux. The ghost-dances had failed to remove the white invaders and the larks had been right when they foretold to the old man that he would die fighting.

By then, Frank and Annie had been with the Wild West Show for seven years and it had lost some of its shine and lustre for them. They decided to take time off to build a house in America – the first real home they had ever had. Nutley in the Eastern state of New Jersey, was the town they chose, and the house was three storeys high with a tower. It cost them $9000, which was a lot of money in those days; but then, not only was Annie a very rich woman by that time, she was good at saving money, too. The Butlers went hunting in New Jersey and had people to dinner, and Annie practised shooting at targets set up on the roof. She was so famous that she was constantly asked to appear in theatres, even the new moving pictures called movies. But, for Annie, the local vaudeville circuit just wasn't the same as the smoke and gunfire of the Wild West and she found it difficult to settle down in one place. Soon she wanted nothing more than to be under canvas again, and on the road with the Wild West Show. It would be another 20 years before the Butlers tried living in a house again.

For the next ten years, Annie continued to work tirelessly. She still had long brown hair, even though she was almost 40, and she looked like a young girl.

But then, in October 1901, disaster struck. The Wild West troupe boarded a three-unit train in Charlotte, North Carolina, to continue its travels and there was a terrible crash. Annie was thrown from her bunk and badly hurt her spine. When she woke up in a hospital bed, her hair had turned completely white. Annie was never the same again and her back caused her pain for the rest of her life. The next year she left the Wild West Show, finally saying goodbye to her life with Buffalo Bill.

But she didn't stop performing. She was now the grand lady of the American shooters and in demand in shows and theatres all over the country. So it wasn't till 1913, when Annie was 48, that she and Frank finally decided to try settling in a house again.

"How about it Annie?" said Frank one day.

"Well... I dunno... " replied Annie, "We've been on the road so long – what would it feel like – bein' in the same place all the time?"

"I reckon it'd be cosy," said Frank, who, being ten years older, was tired of their hectic travelling life.

This time the Butlers decided on a town called Cambridge, in the state of Maryland, where they built a house at the mouth of the Great Choptank River. They had a view from their verandah over the buoys of the oyster fishermen. The town was surrounded by fields where they could hunt. Frank enjoyed the quiet life in Cambridge but Annie, though she tried, still found it difficult to settle in one place. She missed the excitement of life on the road – the people, the surprises, the sound of applause.

Every winter, Annie and Frank went to Leesburg, in Florida, where they shot rattlesnakes and alligators. And it was in Leesburg that Annie sat down and wrote her bestselling autobiography, *Powders I have Used*. There was a steady stream of visitors to Cambridge – some old friends from the Wild West days, and some of Annie's fans who just wanted to get a sight of the most famous woman in America. These were the early days of the movie business, when films were silent and in flickering black and white, and Frank and Annie had many movie actor friends, some of whom, like them, had started out performing on the vaudeville stage.

They bought a dog, a setter called Dave, whom they loved as part of the family – it was as if he were the child they'd never had: they even signed his name, "Dave Butler" on their Christmas cards. Annie claimed that Dave had "almost human intelligence" and, although all her dogs were like children to her, Dave remained the most beloved of all.

In 1914, war broke out in Europe. Germany, led by that very same Kaiser whom Annie had met in Berlin, was the enemy. When America joined the war, Annie, Frank and Dave travelled around the American soldiers' training camps, giving shooting displays and performances to raise the soldiers' spirits. She earned funds for the Red Cross with a stage act in which Dave sniffed out hidden money: it earned him the name *The Red Cross Dog*. Annie was as nimble as she had always been, and, though she now had to wear glasses, she would always hit the bullseye. She performed in charity shows and for special events, skipping into the ring and blowing kisses as if she were sixteen. Annie Oakley could still attract an audience of 100,000 people.

But the 20th century was a different world. America was no longer a land of pioneers: it was the most powerful country in the world. In 1915, Annie and Frank met up with Buffalo Bill again, now old and feeble, a shadow of his former self. He had sold the Wild West Show the year after Annie had left: despite its success, Bill had overspent and he had been in debt ever since. The golden age of the Wild West Show was over: there were by now some 2.5 million radios in America which pumped music and entertainment directly into peoples' own homes.

The war ended in 1918. America was on the winning side, with France and Britain, but in many ways it was left a sadder place. And there was more tragedy to come for Annie, personally.

One day in 1922, the Butlers' chauffeur was driving them to Leesburg for the winter, when they were forced into the sand by a passing vehicle. Frank and Annie got out while their driver tried to push the car out. But rather than push it out he somehow managed to overturn it violently, causing it to fall on top of Annie, and pin her to the ground. Her hip was fractured and her ankle broken. She was in hospital for six weeks. From then on she had a brace on her leg and could walk only short distances. As if that sadness were not enough, the next year Dave died. Annie and Frank were desolate, inconsolable: they buried him in an orange grove in Florida.

By 1924, Annie was 64 years old and Frank 74.

They had been married for almost 50 years and had lived and travelled with the Wild West Show for 30 of them. It felt like the end of the road; it was time, they both decided, to return to the only settled place they could call home – to Annie's own state of Ohio.

The Butlers bought a house in Dayton, a large industrial town, some way from the farming settlements of Greenville and North Star. Annie was Ohio's most famous daughter, the people's favourite heroine, and most days there was a little crowd outside her house wanting autographs.

The railways had brought prosperity to Ohio, it was a now a country of big industry. The forests had been cleared and log cabins like the one that the Moses family had lived in had been replaced by brick houses. Annie felt her body beginning to falter. She knew she was dying and she and Frank together purchased a space in the Mosey family plot in the cemetery in Brock, near Greenville.

By 1926, Annie, feeling weaker and weaker, began to give away her possessions: to her nieces and nephews, she gave the crystal decanter and glasses presented to her by the Kaiser, and a silver tea service, a gift to her from Queen Victoria. The Moses' family moved her to a nursing home in Greenville, but on Wednesday 3rd November, at about eleven o' clock at night, Annie died in her sleep. Frank was too frail to be with her but was looked after by Annie's niece Fern. On hearing the news of Annie's death, he turned his face to the wall and refused to eat another bite. Eighteen days later, he, too, was dead.

***

Frank and Annie are buried together in the cemetery, near Greenville. Two handsome tombstones of red granite mark the spot and read simply: "Annie Oakley and Frank E. Butler at Rest".

It is a peaceful spot, far from the bustle of the city. In the spring, the grass is starred with tiny flowers and the gravestones are shaded by a maple tree. Sometimes a bouquet of flowers lies on the grave, a tribute from somebody who remembers Phoebe Ann Moses, the girl who became Annie Oakley, Watanya Cecilla, Little Sure Shot, America's Queen of Shooters.

GLOSSARY

p.9 **Hickory** – A tree of the walnut family. The wood has a delicious smell when it is burned and the nuts are edible.

p.14 **Buck-eye** – A tree related to the horse chestnut with blue or red flowers.

p.17 **Butternut** – Is also known as the white walnut and is common in the wooded areas of Ohio.

p.21 **Whole-souled** – Means warm-hearted and enthusiastic.

p.24 **Pilchards** – Small, oily fish rather like herrings.

p.25 **Pin money** – Pocket money.

p.25 **Lima beans** – In Britain these are known as broad beans.

p.31 **Crinolines** – Wide skirts, fashionable in the mid nineteenth century, that were fitted over wooden frames that made the material billow out like a round tent.

p.31 **Plunder** – is another word for luggage.

p.32 **Vamoosed** – To "vamoose" is to escape, to run away or vanish.

p.36 **Shyster** – A fraud or a con-man.

p.36 **Comforters** – Long woollen scarves.

p.38 **Linsey** – A piece of coarse linen.

p.39 **Swell** – A wealthy big-shot.

p.39 **Broiled** – (for food) grilled.

p.40 **Bim** – Bang on target.

p.49 **Steer** – A bullock or young bull.

p.49 **Deadwood Stagecoach** – Before the railways, the main form of transport overland was by a passengers stagecoach which was pulled by four of six horses. The town of Deadwood in South Dakota was one of the most important staging posts in the West.

p.52 **Buckskin** – Deerskin. A male deer is called a buck.

p.52 **Gaiters** – These were rather like strong leggings. Often made of leather, wool or cotton, they were tightly buttoned from the knee to right over the feet, fastening under the wearer's shoes.

p.56 **Iron Horse** – When the railways arrived in the West, the native Indians called the train the "Iron Horse".

p.56 **Firewater** – The Indian name for whisky.

p.60 **Brave** – A young warrior was known as a "brave".

p.63 **Broncos** – Half-tame or wild horses which, prior to the correct training, will try to violently buck their rider off the saddle.

p.63 **Tomahawks** – The axe used as a weapon by many Indian warriors.

p.66 **Teepee** – The Plains' Indians lived in cone-shaped buffalo-hide tents that were known as teepees.

p.66 **Corral** – Enclosed area for large numbers of cattle.

p.67 **Moose** – A large animal with antlers which lives in the northern regions of America (also known as an elk).

p.74 **Go mashed upon** – Slang for "fancy".

p.75 **Swanking** – Showing-off, bragging.

RECIPES YOU CAN TRY YOURSELF:

Maple Sugar Candy

This is an Indian recipe from the woods of Ohio where it is known as "snow candy" because the traditional way to make the hot candy harden is to drizzle it on to the snow.

Ingredients:
One and a half teaspoons of butter
240ml of maple syrup

Line a high-sided cake tin with aluminium foil. In a heavy saucepan, met the butter over a medium heat, and when it is melted, add the syrup, stirring constantly. To test that the syrup is ready, take a small amount, about the size of a 5p piece, on the end of a teaspoon and drop it in a saucer of cold water. If it hardens, then it is ready. Quickly pour the syrup onto the aluminium foil in the tin and set aside to cool. When it is quite cold you'll be able to break it into bite-sized pieces.

Hominy Grits

Hominy Grits are roughly ground cornmeal and, in parts of America, especially the southern states, they make a popular breakfast porridge.

Ingredients:
I cup of Hominy Grits
1 teaspoon salt
5 cups of boiling water

Bring the water to the boil and add the salt. Sprinkle the grits on to the water and cook very slowly on a low heat, stirring frequently.

You can eat grits as a savoury, adding gravy and meat, or as a delicious cereal with lots of brown sugar and cream. If you put the leftovers in the fridge, later you can slice them up and fry them in butter.

Key dates

1860: Phoebe Ann Moses is born in Darke County, Ohio
1866: Jacob Moses dies
1868: Annie goes to the Poor Farm in Greenville
1870: Annie goes to live with the Wolves
1872: Annie returns home to her family
1872–4: Annie lives at the Poor Farm in Greenville
1875: Annie beats Frank E. Butler in a shooting match
1876 (though it might have been 1882): Frank Butler and Annie are married
1882: Annie and Frank become a double act and Annie Moses changes her name to Annie Oakley
1884: Annie and Frank join the Sells Brothers Circus
1885: Annie and Frank join Buffalo Bill's Wild West Show
1887: The Wild West Show begins a grand tour of Europe and plays before Queen Victoria for her Golden Jubilee
1888 – 1902: the Butlers tour Europe and America with the Wild West Show
1901: Annie is seriously hurt in a train crash
1902: the Butlers leave the Wild West Show and build a house in Cambridge, Maryland
1914 – 1918: during the First World War, Annie and her dog Dave raise funds for the Red Cross with a touring stage act